IN

EXAMS

F IN EXAMS (2020)

An Hachette UK Company
www.hachette.co.uk

Summersdale Publishers Ltd
Part of Octopus Publishing Group Limited
Carmelite House
50 Victoria Embankment
LONDON
EC4Y 0DZ
UK

www.summersdale.com

Printed and bound in Poland

ISBN: 978-1-78783-568-9

Substantial discounts on bulk quantities of Summersdale books are available to corporations, professional associations and other organizations. For details contact general enquiries: telephone: +44 (0) 1243 771107 or email: enquiries@summersdale.com.

F IN EXAMS

**Even More of the Best
Test Paper Blunders**

Richard Benson

summersdale

Contents

Introduction

Pick up your pens and put on your thinking caps, because school is back in session! Or rather, *F in Exams* is back with its textbook selection of the most shocking, hilarious and unconventional exam answers ever devised. Whether they're blundering through business studies or making serious miscalculations in maths, these resourceful students don't let accuracy get in the way of their creative flair.

If exams were marked on ingenuity, these answers would be top of the class!

Subject: ....**Science**.................

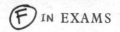

What are two risks of being exposed to high levels of UV radiation?

1. You'll start to glow in the dark.
2. You will interfere with the TV reception if you sit too close.

What are the two products of photosynthesis?

A photo.

A synthesiser (circa 1984).

Human embryos can be used in medical treatments in a process known as therapeutic cloning. What are two disadvantages of therapeutic cloning?

1. It might create a better version of yourself, and everyone will like them more.

2. Having two of the same person - two Donald Trumps, for example.

What type of cell has a permanent vacuole structure?

A prison cell.

Figure 1 shows part of the structure of calcium oxide (CaO).

Figure 1

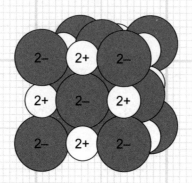

What type of bonding is present in calcium oxide?

Superglue.

Give two examples of elements that are part of the halogen group.

1. Halos.

2. Generator.

Gonorrhoea is a disease caused by a bacterium and can be treated with antibiotics. What other ways could the spread of gonorrhoea be controlled?

A seatbelt.

The resistance band stores elastic potential energy.
What happens when the energy is released?

The person you're aiming at gets a
really red mark.

What are the three types of cable found in standard three-core electrical cable?

1. Cable core 1.

2. Cable core 2.

3. Cable core 3.

Give two safety precautions you should take when performing an experiment using a Bunsen burner?

1. Don't fart (might be explosive).

2. Don't suck on the gas tube.

What forces act on a lorry when the brakes are applied?

TRUCKER-FOOT FORCE.

How does the arrangement of water particles alter when it changes from a solid to a liquid?

It gets **wetter.**

Draw a simple circuit diagram showing a circuit that includes a switch, a lamp and two batteries.

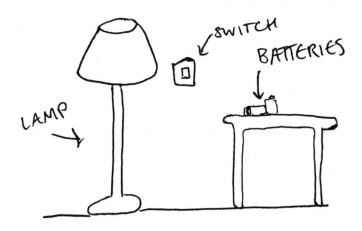

Complete the sentences below.

For many uses, pure iron is too

Ironey.

For many uses, iron from the blast furnace is too

Hot.

Mixtures of iron with carbon are called

Carbiron.

On average, what speed do tectonic plates move at?

About the same as tectonic cups, saucers and bowls.

Subject: **English Language and Literature**

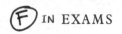

What role does setting play in *The Great Gatsby*?

I don't remember any character called Setting???

Give an example of how aggression between the Capulets and Montagues is presented in Act 1 Scene 1 of *Romeo and Juliet*?

IT'S PRESENTED IN WORDS.

What are some of the major themes explored in *To Kill a Mockingbird*?

Birds.
Murder.

In what ways does Robert Louis Stevenson show the contrast between Dr Jekyll and Mr Hyde through physical descriptions?

Dr Jekyll has a white coat and a ~~test~~ tube.

In what ways does George Orwell use anthropomorphism in *Animal Farm*?

He uses it in the way that anthropomorphism is meant to be used.

Analyse the evolution of the author's presentation of Abel Magwitch in Charles Dickens' *Great Expectations*.

It gets better as the book progresses because Charles Dickens had more experience of writing by the end of the book (It's really long).

"School should only be compulsory up to the age of fourteen."

Give two points arguing either for or against the above statement.

FOR.

1. I wouldn't be sitting in this stupid exam.

2. I could be doing something cool like being a pilot or being Instagram famous.

What device does Cervantes use to introduce the comedic nature of Don Quixote?

A tickling stick.

What is the main theme of John Keats' poem "Ode on a Grecian Urn"?

Urns, and how they are especially nice when they are from Greece.

In Simon Armitage's poem "Mother, any distance greater than a single span", what imagery is used to express the mother-child relationship?

Baby pictures.

How does the structure of Wilfred Owen's "Dulce et Decorum Est" express the mood of the poem?

If you squint your eyes and look at the lines with your head on one side, it looks like a sad face.

Name two techniques a writer can use to convince a reader when writing persuasively.

1. CAPITAL LETTERS.

2. Exclamation marks!!!!

"Public libraries should close permanently."
Give two points arguing either for or against the above statement.

1. The internet knows everything anyway.
2. If we close libraries we'd have more space for Nandos restaurants.

Outline the different attitudes to learning that Bennett presents in *The History Boys*.

He shows that History should only be taught to Boys.

What is the purpose of a prologue?

It's the better version of analogue.

Subject: **Maths**

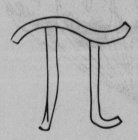

Maths

If it takes 5 apples to make a pie, how many pies can you make with 110 apples?

Depends on the size of your oven.

Alastair, Priyanka and Noah are given £200 by their grandmother.
They are instructed to share the money in a 6:4:3 ratio.
What does Noah get?

A Snickers and some Lego.

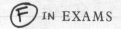

George went for a bike ride. Below is a distance-time graph that plots his full journey.
How long was George stationary for?

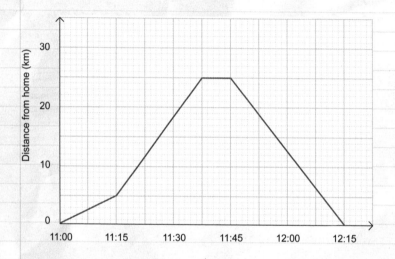

Not very long, he must have been tired by the end.

Maths

Circle the numbers that are multiples of 4 or 6:

12, 2(4) 3(6)   5, 10, 15   9, 10, 11

A holiday costs £125 for a child and three times as much for an adult. How much for two adults and two children to go on this holiday?

If the adults are small, they could maybe pass for children?

Dev's class were given a science test at school. Out of 20 marks, he scored 12, Brendan scored 5, Sienna scored 18 and Dean scored 2. What is the mean score?

The score you get when your teacher doesn't like you.

A fruit bowl contains six bananas, five oranges and two apples. If you choose a fruit from the bowl without looking what per cent chance is there of you picking a banana?

You should 100% be able to tell from the shape.

If Jasmin's train is at 7.14 a.m. and it takes her 25 minutes to get to the station from her home and 5 minutes to buy a ticket, at what time does she need to leave her house?

yesterday?

A swimming pool is 3 metres wide, 9 metres long and 2 metres deep. What is the volume of the swimming pool?

There is a volume of water, then a volume of people within it, and sometimes there are other things, like floaters.

 IN EXAMS

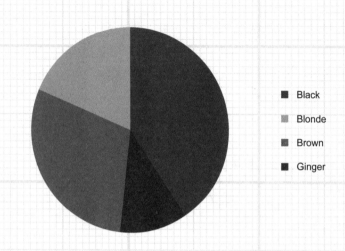

Black
Blonde
Brown
Ginger

The pie chart above shows the hair colour of children in Amy's class. What is the modal hair colour?

It depends on the modal. Cara Delevingne has blonde hair but Kendall Jenner has brown hair.

32

Maths

If the average temperature in December is half the average temperature in April, and the average temperature in April is two thirds of the average temperature in June, what is the average temperature in December if the average temperature in June is 19°C?

Probably a lot colder than June.

Jack and Selena go out to lunch. They each buy a sandwich for £3.50 and Selena buys them both a drink each for £1.20 and a cookie each for 90p. How much does Selena pay?

If they got a meal deal the cost would be the same.

What is the name of this shape?

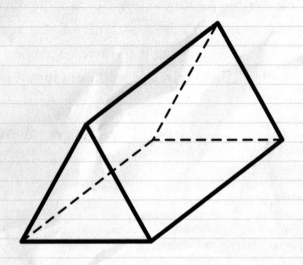

FOUR - PERSON TENT

Subject: **Geography**

The graph below shows changes in the world's urban and rural population from 1970 to 2070 (predicted).

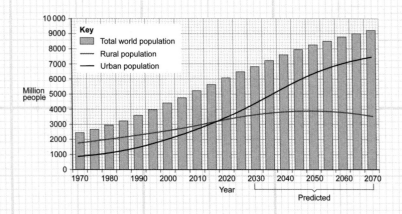

What two statements can you conclude from the above graph about population?

There are now more business people than farmers.

In a couple of hundred years we might run out of farmers.

Geography

Give two examples of renewable energy sources.

1 . Human farts .

2 . Cow farts .

Give two examples of non-renewable energy sources.

1. When your batteries run out.

2. When your light bulb goes out.

How does tourism both positively and negatively impact a country?

Negative: Tourists make you jealous that you're not on holiday.

Positive: Everyone is happier when they are on holiday, so it makes the locals happier too.

Give two things that can be done to help protect the rainforest.

1. Give trees a hug.

2. Leave it alone.

Geography

The photo shows a town that has been flooded.
What are some economic impacts of flooding?

More tourism, as it looks like Venice,
and it has less economic impact now
a lot of money is waterproof.

Give a definition of the term "urban sprawl".

It's when there's a fight in the town centre.

Name one of the measurements that the Human Development Index bases its values on.

BEING KIND.

Geography

"Every year, global weather is getting more and more extreme."
Give evidence to support the above statement.

The statement is in this test, so it must be true. Otherwise, why would it be in here?

Give two ways in which increasing an area's public transport infrastructure impacts the area's ecosystem.

1. Pigeons can sit on bus shelters.

2. More chance of bugs hitting windscreens.

Give an example of a hot desert.

Sticky toffee pudding.

Subject: **History**

In what circumstances did the League of Nations end
and the United Nations begin?

When football became really
popular.

Where did the Great Fire of London begin?

In London.

Who became the monarch of England after the death of Elizabeth I, who had no children?

Elizabeth I's successor.

What are believed to be the causes of the Great Depression?

When loads of people got really sad.

Give an account of the main conflicts faced by Henry VIII during his reign.

One or two Marital troubles.
Coming to terms with being only the eighth best Henry.

When was the NHS introduced in the UK?

When people first started getting sick.

History

What led Henry VIII to carry out the Dissolution of the Monasteries?

When he realized that liquids could be dissolved, he wanted to try it on people.

Give two possible reasons for the start of the French Revolution.

ONION SHORTAGE.

BAGUETTE SCARCITY.

What effect did Viking expansion have on the areas they reached?

Big hats with horns became more popular.

What were Victorian workhouses used for?

To keep all the Victorians busy.

Which leader introduced China's Cultural Revolution?

Jackie Chan.

Give two reasons for the outbreak of the American Civil War.

1. Arguments about who deserved to win the Superbowl.
2. President Trump's plans to build a wall to block Mexico.

What was a key event that escalated the conflict leading to the Vietnam War?

The Human Missile Crisis.

Who fought in the Hundred Years' War?

Old people, if it lasted 100 years.

History

Where was William the Conqueror born?

He was born in Conquer,
making him a Conqueror
(I was born in London,
so I'm a Londoner).

Describe the events of Custer's defeat at the Battle of
Little Big Horn.

THEY COULDN'T AGREE ON WHETHER THE HORN
WAS BIG OR LITTLE AND THEN
SOMEONE STABBED HIM WITH IT.

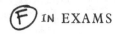

What effect did the reduction in the use of capital punishment have on the British prison system in the nineteenth century?

Everyone had to write in small letters.

What were two outcomes of the fall of the Berlin Wall?

1. Less Wall.
2. Reduction in graffiti.

Subject: **Business Studies**

ROAD TO SUCCESS

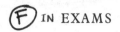

Why might a sole trader decide to have a partner join their business?

Selling shoes is tough on your own.

Why should a business endeavour to have an efficient and effective recruitment and hiring process?

Because you don't want to accidentally hire someone who is really bad.

Give an example of an asset.

Good Looks.

What could a business do to encourage external growth?

Plant some trees outside their office.

Describe the difference between a flat and a tall organizational structure.

One is made up of bungalows, the other skyscrapers.

Give an example of a stakeholder.

BUFFY THE VAMPIRE SLAYER.

What is the Boston Matrix?

It's a bit like a
Rubiks cube.

What is the difference between quantitative and qualitative market research?

You have to pick whether you prefer quality of research or quantity of research.

Give an example of a business in the tertiary sector.

Pet shops for turtles.

How could outsourcing benefit a business?

You can get everyone else to do your work for you.

What is price skimming and why would a company do it?

It's like stone skimming, so a company would only do it if they were near a lake.

Give an example of a group that would benefit from higher interest rates.

Any social media group that has like 10 or 12 followers on social media needs higher interest rates.

What is an economic resource? Give two examples.

1. Solar power.
2. Re-usable shopping bags.

Define the term monopoly.

A BORING BOARD GAME THAT TAKES
AGES TO FINISH.

Give an example of a time when the government would intervene in a specific industry?

The government are always intervening in my uncle's herbal gardening business, sending round the police and confiscating his crops!

Summarize the basic economic problem.

I don't have enough money.

Subject: **Government & Politics**

How can legislation be used to regulate the environment?

WE CAN BAN SQUIRRELS FROM TAKING FOOD FROM THE FEEDERS. THAT FOOD IS NOT MEANT FOR THEM AND IT'S JUST MEAN.

Ideologically, what are the reasons for progressive teaching methods?

Teaching Students about the Positives of gressives.

Discuss the opinion that right-wing governments are more economically competent than left-wing governments.

More people are right-handed than left-handed, so they're better. And I guess it's the same with birds.

Explain the relation between the three branches of government in the US.

They're all from the same tree.

What are the dangers of a politicized judiciary?

If the judiciary becomes too polite they won't send anyone to jail!

What is the difference between social liberalism and economic liberalism?

Social Liberals want friends and economic Liberals want money.

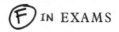
What are the roles of the chief whips in the UK Parliament?

Contolling the mounted police horses.

What is the difference between the U(S) and U(K) constitution?

THESE LETTERS.

How does the concept of direct democracy work?

You just have to be more up front about your democracy and not be ashamed of it.

How do pressure groups pursue their aims?

They do a lot of squeezing.

Define the term "safe seat".

One with a belt. And an airbag in front.

How can referendums undermine or enhance democracy?

Idiots are allowed to vote. And there are a lot of idiots out there.

What is the US Electoral College and how does it work?

It's an American college and it works by electric.

Give an example of why an organization would donate to a political party?

The party might need money to buy balloons, party snacks and fizzy drinks.

What is the difference between cultural and economic globalization?

One is a globe with a yoghurt on and the other is a globe with money on.

What are some potential global superpowers?

Wakanda.

How did the European Union develop from the European Economic Community?

They changed a few words in their name.

Why do some people believe there should be a "benefit cap"?

A benefit cap could help you keep the sun out of your eyes in summer and keep your head warm in winter.

Subject: **Music**

What Italian word is used to denote a lively and fast tempo?

Pesto.

What does polyrhythmic mean?

Singing parrots.

What feeling does the use of a major chord give to a piece of music?

♡ALL the Feels.♡

What term is used to instruct the performer to play loudly?

"Louder!"

Music

What is the vocal technique of singing notes above the performer's normal range?

Screaming.

Give three instruments in the woodwind family.

1. Oak flute.
2. Beech whistle.
3. Pine piccolo.

What is the musical term for a repeated rhythmic pattern?

Boring.

What are the features of a pentatonic melody?

It's when you practice the occult to music.

What do dynamics tell you about how to play a piece of music?

When to let off explosives.

What does a quarter rest mean?

It means that you can have a little rest, but not a big sleep

How would you describe the melody of Beethoven's "Für Elise"?

Pretty good.

What are some characteristics of music from the Romantic period?

1. Big hair.

2. Frilly shirts.

In the time signature 6/8, how many beats are in a measure?

Half a pint.

What effect does a natural sign have on a note?

It's printed using recycled paper.

What musical term means a strong attack?

CHARGE!!!

Draw a sharp sign.

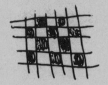

Subject: **Psychology**

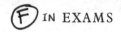
What are the psychological reasons for people conforming?

They're scared of going to prison.

What is the working memory model?

YOUR BRAIN.

How can animals be used in an ethical way to study attachment?

You have to ask them nicely first.

Define the cognitive approach to psychology.

It's the same as psychology but with cogs instead of brains.

Explain how social influence processes contribute to social change.

When YouTubers show off a product in a video and suddenly everyone else buys it too.

What are the benefits of the biological approach when compared to the behaviourist approach?

More cute animals, less silly rules.

What is systematic desensitization?

A really good score in Scrabble.

What differences are there between the autonomic nervous system and the somatic nervous system?

They are both terrified, but terrified of different things.

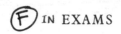

Why is the "fight or flight" response less useful to modern humans than our ancestors?

Because we can't fly anymore. We can only fight.

What is meant by the term "pilot study"?

What you have to do to pass your exams if you want to fly a plane.

Psychology

In psychopathology, how could flooding be used to treat a phobia?

You distract your patient from their fears by flooding their home.

How can obsessions and compulsions affect a person's life?

It means you won't stop until you catch all the Pokémon.

Outline one strength and one weakness with a strongly deterministic view?

Strength: your determinism is strong.
Weakness: your strength is determinism.

Argue which is more problematic out of alpha bias and beta bias.

If you're going to be biased it might as well be alphabetically, so beta.

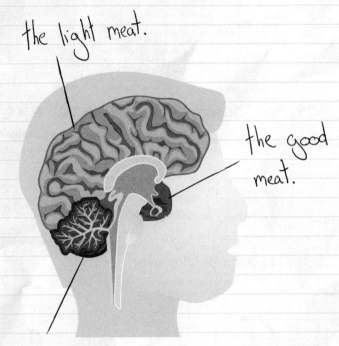

the light meat.

the good meat.

the dark meat.

Label this diagram of the head's endocrine glands.

What are investigator effects?

STROBE LIGHTS FOR PRIVATE EYES.

Demonstrate an element of Freud's psychoanalytic theory of gender development.

Subject: **Religious Studies**

What do Catholics believe about life after death?

That the Pope is somehow involved.

What is "dāna" in Buddhism?

What's dāna is dāna, as they say.

Religious Studies

Give two examples of how a Christian may perform worship.

1. On a stage
2. On TV

How do Hindus respond to suffering?

By saying "Ouch!" like any other person.

What was promised to Abraham by God in the Covenant?

that he would win the American Civil War.

Why were Adam and Eve banished from the Garden of Eden?

Littering.

Religious Studies

In one belief system of your choice, explain how beliefs are more important than actions.

If beliefs weren't real, I wouldn't be able to be a Belieber, which is super important to me.

Explain why Bar Mitzvah ceremonies are important to Jews.

Because they like having alcoholic drinks, so having a mitzvah at a bar is ideal.

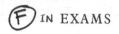

In Buddhism, why is the Eightfold Path important?

The other seven paths led nowhere good.

Referring to a source of wisdom and authority, discuss how music is used to express Christian beliefs.

Jesus used to play guitar and sing prayers.

What is the Hindu concept of Prakṛti?

Prakṛti makes perfekti.

What are the five Ks in Sikhism?

Kim, Kylie, Kourtney, Khloe and Kendall

Discuss how one religion is committed to its holy book.

Potter fans keep buying whatever J.K. Rowling puts out.

How might a pilgrimage benefit someone spiritually?

Long walks out in the air make people feel better.

Give two different types of meditation.

Aspirin + paracetamol.

Explain how a Creation account contributes to the belief system of one religion.

People who believe in religion bank-transfer money into its creation account to help raise funds for it.

Subject: **Classical Studies**

In what ways did Athenian citizens get involved in running the city of Athens?

They had a cake sale to raise some money.

How do classical texts generally look on the idea of fate? Give an example.

There are many examples of fates in classical texts, because bouncy castles and face painting didn't exist to raise money for schools.

What opportunities were there for making a living in Pompeii?

Selling bags of volcanic ash.

What type of settlement was Vindolanda?

They specialised in curry.

In Ancient Greece, what would affect the auction price of a slave?

If they came with their own toga.

Explain the relationship between Ancient Greece and the modern idea of democracy?

They voted. We vote. Not much else to say.

Name the central figure in the above sculpture.

RUSSELL CROWE.

Give an argument for one possible identity of Homer.

He had to dress up as Krusty in at least one episode.

Justify why *Oedipus Rex* is classified as a tragedy.

It's Sad that all the dinosaurs died. ☹

What is this building in Rome called?

The bus depot.

What does Juvenal's *Satires* tell us about Roman society?

I chose not to read this book, because I don't think we should be reading stuff for juveniles.

Describe one way in which a conflict is resolved in a classical text.

Everyone has a good time at a toga party and forgets about it.

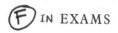

What was the relationship of Pliny the Elder and Pliny the Younger?

It's the same person at different ages.

Name one of the 12 Labours of Hercules.

WASHING DISHES.

Subject: **Drama**

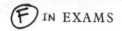

What is meant when a performance is said to be "in the round"?

It's quite trendy because it's not square.

How can an actor use physical skills to portray a character? Give an example.

Physically write their lines on their hands so they don't forget them.

What are the benefits of a one-act play over a two-act play?

Fewer lines to remember.

Discuss *Death of a Salesman*'s presentation of the American dream.

1. First you work...
2. ... then you die.

What are the benefits and weaknesses of using scenery on a wheeled platform, as pictured above?

Benefits: spinning around.

weakness: people falling off and injuring themselves if you spin too fast.

What are some of the issues that might be encountered when adapting a novel into a play?

The actors having to wait while you turn the pages of the book.

How can lighting give a sense of atmosphere in a stage production?

People start to wake up (there is more atmosphere) when the lights come back on and the show has finished.

In what ways can a director establish a sense of time and place in a production?

Having a character mention where and when they are in the first line: "How are you today, here in London, in the year 1852?"

How are illusion and fantasy central themes of *A Streetcar Named Desire*?

It's fiction, so it's all an illusion.

In what ways can pacing be used to make a play more effective?

If the show gets boring, the actors should pace around the stage to keep the attention of the audience.

Give an example of a play you have seen that uses a blackout effectively.

One that had a powercut halfway through.

What are the benefits of performing a play on a raked stage?

It means there are less leaves that the cast might slip on.

How much can Henrik Ibsen's *A Doll's House* be a considered a "realist" play?

The dolls they used were very life-like.

Why might a production make use of a black-box theatre space?

If the show is about an aeroplane.

What might attract an actor to performing in Harold Pinter's *A Birthday Party*?

They love balloons and there's free cake every night.

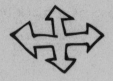

Subject: **Technology + Design**

Imagine the possible process that went into the designing of the chair pictured above.

Going to IKEA, looking at other chairs and copying them.

Give an example of a material that should not be used outdoors without a protective coating?

Skin.

How is plywood manufactured?

Chop down plywood trees, saw into planks.

What is the environmental impact of using glass bottles instead of Tetra-Paks?

GLASS IS HEAVIER, SO IT WEIGHS THE WORLD DOWN MORE, MEANING IT COULD CRASH INTO THE SUN.

Define just-in-time manufacturing.

Better than late manufacturing.

Draw the logo which indicates that a product can be recycled.

RECYCLABLE

What is the bias on a piece of fabric?

Most people like denim, but hardly anyone likes corduroy.

What are the benefits of using microfibre?

Superfast broadband.

What would be the most appropriate way to print a mass-produced greetings card?

With a big printer.

Give two examples of situations where it would be appropriate to use ear protectors.

1. When it's really cold outside.
2. When you don't want to hear your dad's snoring.

You've been asked by a gaming peripherals company to design a gaming chair. Draw and describe your design below.

Technology + Design

Give examples of products that would and would not be appropriate for injection moulding production.

WOULD: oranges.

WOULD NOT: balloons.

What is reforestation and why is it important?

When you watch Forrest Gump twice in a row because it teaches you a lot about life.

What are some uses for HIPS (High Impact Polystyrene)?

SHAKIRA HAS A LOT OF USES FOR HERS.

Give a production task that would require the use of a lathe?

Washing your hands – you have to do it for 20 seconds, or as long as it takes to sing the chorus of "Living on a Prayer".

THE WORLD'S
BEST JOKES (THAT
YOU'LL REMEMBER)

Unforgettable Jokes and
Gags for All the Family

James Briggs

£9.99
Hardback
ISBN: 978-1-78783-570-2

**Would you like to hear my song about tortillas?
Actually, it's more of a rap.**

Prepare to have your sides split and your ribs tickled
in this ultimate collection of the world's most
memorable jokes! This seriously silly compendium of
unforgettable one-liners, catchy quips and everything
in-between is sure to have the whole family aching
with laughter. Giggle fits guaranteed!

If you're interested in finding out more about our books, find us on Facebook at **Summersdale Publishers** and follow us on Twitter at @**Summersdale**.

www.summersdale.com

Image Credits

p.12 – © Jasminko Ibrakovic/Shutterstock.com; p.14 – © Rob Wilson/Shutterstock.com; p.28 – © attaphong/Shutterstock.com; p.39 – © Matej Kastelic/Shutterstock.com; p.42 – © apstockphoto/Shutterstock.com; p.89 – © Designua/Shutterstock.com; p.104 – © Photo Oz/Shutterstock.com; p.106 – © Phant/Shutterstock.com; p.112 – © Kozlik/Shutterstock.com; p.119 – © Alexander Tolstykh/Shutterstock.com